thisconnectionofeveryonewithlungs

NEW CALIFORNIA POETRY

EDITED BY

Robert Hass
Calvin Bedient
Brenda Hillman
Forrest Gander

thisconnectionof

julianaspahr

everyonewithlungs

poems

UNIVERSITY OF CALIFORNIA PRESS / BERKELEY LOS ANGELES LONDON

University of California Press
Berkeley and Los Angeles, California

University of California Press, Ltd.
London, England

Library of Congress Cataloging-in-Publication Data

Spahr, Juliana.
    This connection of everyone with lungs : poems / Juliana Spahr.
        p.   cm. — (New California Poetry ; 15)
        ISBN-13 978-0-520-24295-1 (pbk. : alk. paper)
        ISBN-10 0-520-24295-5 (pbk. : alk. paper)
    1. September 11 Terrorist Attacks, 2001—Poetry.   2. Victims of
terrorism—Poetry.   3. Protest poetry, American.   4. Terrorism—
Poetry.   I. Title. II. Series.

PS3569.P3356T46   2005
811'.54—dc22   2004008292

Manufactured in Canada
15   14   13   12   11   10   09   08
11   10   9   8   7   6   5   4

The paper used in this publication meets the minimum require-
ments of ANSI / NISO Z39.48-1992 (R 1997) (*Permanence of Paper*).

Thank yous to Bill Luoma and Charles Weigl
for all sorts of help with these poems. Thanks also
to Ida Yoshinaga for her associative critiques.

CONTENTS

ACKNOWLEDGMENTS

Versions of these poems have previously
appeared or will appear in various magazines.

"Poem Written after September 11" appeared
with the title "Poem" in *Lit* 6 (2002).

"December 2, 2002" and "December 3, 2002"
appeared in *The Baffler* 16 (2003).

"December 1, 2002," "December 4, 2002,"
"January 13, 2003," "January 20, 2003,"
"January 28, 2003," "February 15, 2003,"
"March 5, 2003," "March 11, 2003," and
"March 16, 2003" appeared in *syllogism* 6
(2004).

"March 17, 2003" appeared in the *Village Voice*
(May 21–27, 2003).

"March 27 and 30, 2003" appeared in *War and
Peace* (Oakland: O Books, 2004).

"November 30, 2002" and "December 8,
2002" appeared in *Bomb Magazine* (summer
2004).

poemwrittenafterseptember11/2001

There are these things:

cells, the movement of cells and the division of cells

and then the general beating of circulation

and hands, and body, and feet

and skin that surrounds hands, body, feet.

This is a shape,

a shape of blood beating and cells dividing.

But outside of this shape is space.

There is space between the hands.

There is space between the hands and space around the hands.

There is space around the hands and space in the room.

There is space in the room that surrounds the shapes of everyone's hands and body and feet and cells and the beating contained within.

There is space, an uneven space, made by this pattern of bodies.

This space goes in and out of everyone's bodies.

Everyone with lungs breathes the space in and out as everyone with lungs breathes the space between the hands in and out

as everyone with lungs breathes the space between the hands and
the space around the hands in and out

as everyone with lungs breathes the space between the hands and
the space around the hands and the space of the room in and out

as everyone with lungs breathes the space between the hands and
the space around the hands and the space of the room and the
space of the building that surrounds the room in and out

as everyone with lungs breathes the space between the hands and
the space around the hands and the space of the room and the
space of the building that surrounds the room and the space of
the neighborhoods nearby in and out

as everyone with lungs breathes the space between the hands and
the space around the hands and the space of the room and the
space of the building that surrounds the room and the space of
the neighborhoods nearby and the space of the cities in and out

as everyone with lungs breathes the space between the hands
and the space around the hands and the space of the room and
the space of the building that surrounds the room and the space
of the neighborhoods nearby and the space of the cities and the
space of the regions in and out

as everyone with lungs breathes the space between the hands
and the space around the hands and the space of the room and
the space of the building that surrounds the room and the space
of the neighborhoods nearby and the space of the cities and the
space of the regions and the space of the nations in and out

as everyone with lungs breathes the space between the hands
and the space around the hands and the space of the room and
the space of the building that surrounds the room and the space
of the neighborhoods nearby and the space of the cities and the
space of the regions and the space of the nations and the space of
the continents and islands in and out

as everyone with lungs breathes the space between the hands
and the space around the hands and the space of the room and

the space of the building that surrounds the room and the space
of the neighborhoods nearby and the space of the cities and the
space of the regions and the space of the nations and the space
of the continents and islands and the space of the oceans in and
out

as everyone with lungs breathes the space between the hands
and the space around the hands and the space of the room and
the space of the building that surrounds the room and the space
of the neighborhoods nearby and the space of the cities and the
space of the regions and the space of the nations and the space
of the continents and islands and the space of the oceans and the
space of the troposphere in and out

as everyone with lungs breathes the space between the hands
and the space around the hands and the space of the room and
the space of the building that surrounds the room and the space
of the neighborhoods nearby and the space of the cities and the
space of the regions and the space of the nations and the space
of the continents and islands and the space of the oceans and the
space of the troposphere and the space of the stratosphere in and
out

as everyone with lungs breathes the space between the hands and the space around the hands and the space of the room and the space of the building that surrounds the room and the space of the neighborhoods nearby and the space of the cities and the space of the regions and the space of the nations and the space of the continents and islands and the space of the oceans and the space of the troposphere and the space of the stratosphere and the space of the mesosphere in and out.

In this everything turning and small being breathed in and out by everyone with lungs during all the moments.

Then all of it entering in and out.

The entering in and out of the space of the mesosphere in the entering in and out of the space of the stratosphere in the entering in and out of the space of the troposphere in the entering in and out of the space of the oceans in the entering in and out of the space of the continents and islands in the entering in and out of the space of the nations in the entering in and out of the space of the regions in the entering in and out of the space of the cities in the entering in and out of the space of the neighborhoods nearby in the entering in and out of the space of the building in the entering in and out of the space of the room in the entering in and out of the space around the hands in the entering in and out of the space between the hands.

How connected we are with everyone.

The space of everyone that has just been inside of everyone mixing inside of everyone with nitrogen and oxygen and water vapor and argon and carbon dioxide and suspended dust spores and bacteria mixing inside of everyone with sulfur and sulfuric acid and titanium and nickel and minute silicon particles from pulverized glass and concrete.

How lovely and how doomed this connection of everyone with lungs.

Brooklyn, New York

poemwrittenfromnovember30/2002
tomarch27/2003

Note . . .

After September 11, I kept thinking that the United States wouldn't invade Afghanistan. I was so wrong about that.

So on November 30, 2002, when I realized that it was most likely that the United States would invade Iraq again, I began to sort through the news in the hope of understanding how this would happen. I thought that by watching the news more seriously I could be a little less naive. But I gained no sophisticated understanding as I wrote these poems.

September 11 shifted my thinking in this way. The constant attention to difference that so defines the politics of Hawai'i, the disconnection that Hawai'i claims at moments with the continental United States, felt suddenly unhelpful. I felt I had to think about what I was connected with, and what I was complicit with, as I lived off the fat of the military-industrial complex on a small island. I had to think about my intimacy with things I would rather not be intimate with even as (because?) I was very far away from all those things geographically. This feeling made lyric—with its attention to connection, with its dwelling on the beloved and on the afar—suddenly somewhat poignant, somewhat apt, even somewhat more useful than I usually find it.

November 30, 2002

Beloveds, we wake up in the morning to darkness and watch it turn into lightness with hope.

Each morning we wait in our bed listening for the parrots and their chattering.

Beloveds, the trees branch over our roof, over our bed, and so realize that when I speak about the parrots I speak about love and their green colors, love and their squawks, love and the discord they bring to the calmness of morning, which is the discord of waking.

When I speak of the parrots I speak of all that we wake to this morning, the Dow slipping yet still ending in a positive mood yesterday, Mission Control, the stalled railcar in space, George Harrison's extra-large will, Hare Krishnas, the city of Man, the city of Danane and the Movement for Justice and Peace and the Ivorian Popular Movement for the Great West, homelessness and failed coups, few leads in the bombing in Kenya.

Today I still speak of the fourteen that are dead in Kenya from earlier in the week, some by their own choice and some by the choices of others, as I speak of the parrots.

And as I speak of the parrots I speak of the day's weather here, the slight breeze and the blanket I pull over myself this morning in the subtropics and then I speak also of East Africa, those detained for questioning, porous borders, the easy availability of fraudulent passports.

I speak of long coastlines and Alexandre Dumas's body covered in blue cloth with the words "all for one, one for all."

I speak of grandsons of black Haitian slaves and what it means to be French.

I speak of global jihad, radical clerics, giant planets, Jupiter, stars' gas and dust, gravitational accretion, fluid dynamics, protoplanetary evolution, the unstoppable global spread of AIDS.

When I speak of the parrots I speak of the pair of pet conures released sometime in 1986 or 1987 that now number at least thirty.

I speak of how they begin their day at sunrise and fly at treetop
height southward to rest in the trees near our bed, beloveds, where
they rest for about an hour to feed, preen, and socialize before
moving on to search for fruits and seeds of wild plum, Christmas
berry, papaya, strawberry guava, and other shrubs and trees that
were, like them, like us, brought here from somewhere else.

I speak of our morning to come, mundane with the news of it all,
with its hour of feeding, preening, and restrained socializing
before turning to our separate computers and the wideness of
their connections and the probable hourly changes of temperature
between 79 and 80 degrees that will happen all day long with
winds that begin the day at 12 mph and end it at 8 mph.

When I speak of the green of the parrots I speak of yous and me,
beloveds, and our roosts at the bottom of the crater once called
Lēʻahi, now called Diamond Head, and I speak of those who
encourage us to think of them as roosting with us, Mariah Carey,
Jermaine Dupri, Jimmy Jam and Terry Lewis, Jay-Z, Cam'ron,
Justin Timberlake, Nick Carter, Rod Stewart, and Shania Twain.

And I speak of the flapping of parrots' wings as they come over the tree that reaches over the bed and the helpless flapping of our wings in our mind, our wings flapping as we are on our backs in our bed at night unable to turn over or away from this, the three-legged stool of political piece, military piece, and development piece, that has entered into our bed at night holding us down sleepless as the parrots have entered into this habitat far away from their origin because someone set them free, someone set them free, and they fly from one place to another, loudly, to remind us of our morning and we welcome this even, stuck on our backs in bed, wings flapping, welcome any diversion from the pieces of the three-legged stool.

December 1, 2002

Beloveds, yours skins is a boundary separating yous from the rest of yous.

When I speak of skin I speak of the largest organ.

I speak of the separations that define this world and the separations that define us, beloveds, even as we like to press our skins against one another in the night.

When I speak of skin I speak of lighting candles to remember AIDS and the history of attacks in Kenya.

I speak of toxic fumes given off by plastic flooring in a burning nightclub in Caracas.

I speak of the forty-seven dead in Caracas.

And I speak of the four dead in Palestine.

And of the three dead in Israel.

I speak of those dead in other parts of the world who go unreported.

I speak of boundaries and connections, locals and globals, butterfly wings and hurricanes.

I speak of one hundred and fifty people sheltering at the Catholic Mission in the city of Man.

I speak of a diverted Ethiopian airliner, US attacks on Iraqi air defense sites, and warnings not to visit Yemen.

Here, where we are with our separate skins polished by sweet-smelling soaps and the warm, clean water of our shower, we sit in our room in the morning and the sounds of birds are outside our windows and the sun shines.

When I speak of yours skins, I speak of newspaper headlines in other countries and different newspaper headlines here.

I speak of how the world suddenly seems as if it is a game of some sort, a game where troops are massed on a flat map of the world and if one looks at the game board long enough one can see the patterns even as one is powerless to prevent them.

I speak of the memory of the four floating icebergs off the coast of Argentina and the thirty thousand dead salmon in the Klamath River this year.

I speak of how I cannot understand our insistence on separations and how these separations have nothing and everything to do with the moments when we feel joined and separated from each others.

I speak of the intimate relationship between salmons and humans, between humans and icebergs, between icebergs and salmons, and how this is just the beginning of the circular list.

I speak of those moments when we do not understand why we must remain separated or joined only in the most mundane ways.

I speak of why our skin is our largest organ and how it keeps us contained.

I speak of the preservation of a balanced internal environment, shock absorbers, temperature regulators, insulators, sensators, lubrications, protections and grips, and body odor.

I speak of the Pew study on anti-Americanism and the three C's of the IRA—Columbia, Castlereagh, and Stormont Castle—and I speak of the unconfirmed dead in Iraq from the bombing of a refinery at Basrah.

When I speak of skin I speak of a slow day in the forces that are compelling all of us to be brushing up against one another.

When I speak of skin I speak of the crowds that are gathering all together to meet each other with various intents.

When I speak of skin I speak of all the movement in the world right now and all the new boundaries of the right now that are made by all the movement in the world right now and then broken by all the movement in the world right now.

But when I speak of skin I do not speak of the arbitrary connotations of color that have made all this brushing against one another even harder for all of us.

Beloveds, yours skins are of all colors, are soft and wrinkled, blotchy and reddish, full of blemish and smooth.

Our world is small, contained within 1.4 to 2 square meters of surface area.

Yet it is all the world that each of us has and so we all return to it, to the softening of it and to the defoliating of it and to the moisture that we bring to it.

December 2, 2002

As it happens every night, beloveds, while we turned in the night sleeping uneasily the world went on without us.

We live in our own time zone and there are only a small million of us in this time zone and the world as a result has a tendency to begin and end without us.

While we turned sleeping uneasily at least ten were injured in a bomb blast in Bombay and four killed in Palestine.

While we turned sleeping uneasily a warehouse of food aid was destroyed, stocks on upbeat sales soared, Australia threatened first strikes, there was heavy gunfire in the city of Man, the Belarus ambassador to Japan went missing, a cruise ship caught fire, on yet another cruise ship many got sick, and the pope made a statement against xenophobia.

While we turned sleeping uneasily perhaps J Lo gave Ben a prenuptial demand for sex four times a week.

While we turned sleeping uneasily Liam Gallagher brawled and irate fans complained that "Popstars: The Rivals" was fixed.

While we turned sleeping uneasily the Supreme Court agreed to hear the case of whether university admissions may favor racial minorities.

While we turned sleeping uneasily poachers caught sturgeon in the reed-fringed Caspian, which shelters boar and wolves, and some of the residents on the space shuttle planned a return flight to the US.

Beloveds, our world is small and isolated.

We live our lives in six hundred square feet about a quarter mile from the shore on land that is seven hundred square miles and five thousand miles from the nearest land mass.

Despite our isolation, there is no escape from the news of how many days are left in the Iraq inspections.

The news poll for today was should we invade Iraq now or should we wait until the inspections are complete and we tried to laugh together at this question but our laughter was uneasy and we just decided to turn off the television that arrives to us from those other time zones.

Beloveds, we do not know how to live our lives with any agency outside of our bed.

It makes me angry that how we live in our bed—full of connected loving and full of isolated sleep and dreaming also—has no relevance to the rest of the world.

How can the power of our combination of intimacy and isolation have so little power outside the space of our bed?

Beloveds, the shuttle is set to return home and out the window of the shuttle one can see the earth.

"How massive the earth is; how minute the atmosphere," one of the astronauts notes.

Beloveds, what do we do but keep breathing as best we can this minute atmosphere?

December 3, 2002

Beloveds, I've said it before, our bed is a few square feet, our
apartment is six hundred square feet, our city is eighty-two square
miles, and we live on land that is seven hundred square miles.

We walk less than a mile to the sixty-four billion square miles of
the Pacific.

Beloveds, today the UN commission searched all the square feet of
Hussein's office in a show of power.

When I speak of feet I speak of attacks conceived in Afghanistan,
planned in Germany, funded through Dubai, executed in America,
using Saudis.

I speak of the frozen assets of Osama bin Laden and the demand
from Turkey for a second UN resolution before the US moves in
on Iraq.

I speak of Ahmed Zakayev being set free and Malaysia warning
Australia that any preemptive strike against them even in the name
of preventing terrorism would be an act of war.

Beloveds, I keep trying to speak of loving but all I speak about is acts of war and acts of war and acts of war.

I mean to speak of beds and bowers and all I speak of is Barghouti's call for a change of leadership and the strike in Venezuela against Chavez and the sixty-six ships on the fleet of shame.

I speak of the sixteen million people from Mali and Burkina Faso who are in the Ivory Coast and their morning possibility of peace that disappears by evening.

I speak of the eighty evacuated from Touba.

I speak of the ninety-five-year-old woman who was shot by Israeli troops while driving her car from Palestine into Israel.

I speak of the six-hundred-year-old Spanish Haggadah now in Sarajevo.

I speak of Burundi and the Forces for the Defense of Democracy.

I speak of the US wanting to ban the antidote to nerve gas on the Oil-Food plan with Iraq.

I speak of the release of Saaduddin Ibrahim and his twenty-seven employees.

I do not say more than movement when I speak. I speak of movements larger than our short walk to the beach and our immersion in the sixty-four billion square miles of cool saltwater once we get there.

Beloveds, we say we do not want to move anymore. We want to see ourselves as located and bound even if not local, located and bound to someone else's land, and there by chance even as we do not see ourselves as part of the land.

This is all we want today

Yet the world swirls around us.

The ocean levels rise and the beach gets smaller.

We say our bed is part of everyone else's bed even as our bed is denied to others by an elaborate system of fences and passport-checking booths.

We wake up in the night with just each others and admit that even while we believe that we want to believe that we all live in one bed of the earth's atmosphere, our bed is just our bed and no one else's and we can't figure out how to stop it from being that way.

December 4, 2002

Embedded deep in our cells is ourselves and everyone else.

Going back ten generations we have nine thousand ancestors and going back twenty-five we get thirty million.

All of us shaped by all of us and then other things as well, other things such as the flora and the fauna and all the other things as well.

When I speak of yours thighs and their long muscles of smoothness, I speak of yours cells and I speak of the British Embassy being closed in Kenya and the US urging more aggressive Iraq inspections and the bushfire that is destroying homes in Sydney.

And I speak of at least one dead after rioting in Dili and the arrest of Mukhlas, and Sharon's offer of 40 percent of the West Bank and the mixed results of Venezuela's oil strike and the overtures that Khatami is making to the US.

When I speak of the curve of yours cheeks, their soft down, their cell after cell, their smoothness, their even color, I speak of the

NASA launch and the child Net safety law and the Native Linux pSeries Server.

When I speak of our time together, I speak also of the new theories of the development of the cell from iron sulfide, formed at the bottom of the oceans.

I speak of the weight of the alien planet.

And I speak of the benefits of swaddling sleeping babies.

Beloveds, all our theories and generations came together today in order to find the optimum way of lacing shoes. The bow tie pattern is the most efficient.

I want to tie everything up when I speak of yous.

I want to tie it all up and tie up the world in an attempt to understand the swirls of patterns.

But there is no efficient way.

The news refreshes every few minutes on the computer screen and on the television screen. The stories move from front to back and then off the page and then perhaps forward again in a motion that I can't predict but I suspect is not telling the necessary truths.

I can't predict our time together either. Or why we like each other like we do.

I have no idea when our bodies will feel very good to one of us or to all of us together or to none of us.

The drive to press against one another that is there at moments and then gone at others.

The drive to press up against others in the same way.

December 8, 2002

Beloveds, those astronauts on the space station began their trip
home a few days ago and sent ahead of them images of the earth
from space.

In space, the earth is a firm circle of atmosphere and the ocean and
the land exist in equilibrium. The forces of nature are in the blue
and the white and the green.

All is quiet.

All the machinery, all the art is in the quiet.

Something in me jumps when I see these images, jumps toward
comfort and my mind settles.

This, I think, is one of the most powerful images in our time of
powers.

Perhaps it isn't lovers in our beds that matter, perhaps it is the
earth.

Not the specific in our bed at night but the globe in our mind, a globe that we didn't see really until the twentieth century, with all its technologies and variations on the mirror.

Beloveds, when we first moved to this island in the middle of the Pacific I took comfort from a postcard of the islands seen from space that I bought in a store in Waikīkī. There was no detail of the buildings of Waikīkī in the islands seen from space. No signs of the brackish Ala Wai that surrounds Waikīkī. Everything looked pristine and sparkled from space. All the machinery, all the art was in the pristine sparkle of the ocean and its kindness to land. The ocean was calm.

Beloveds, this poem is an attempt to speak with the calmness of the world seen from space and to forget the details.

This is an attempt to speak of clouds that appear in endless and beautiful patterns on the surface of the earth and that we see from beneath, out the window from our bed as we lie there in the morning enjoying the touch of each other's bodies.

This is an attempt to speak in praise of the firm touch of yours hands on my breast at night and its comfort to me.

An attempt to celebrate the moments late at night when yous wake up with kindness.

An attempt to speak away.

And when I say this what I mean is that I am attempting to speak to yous of these things in order to get out of our bed in the morning in the face of all that happened and is yet to happen, the spinning earth, the gathering forces of some sort of destruction that is endless and happens over and over, each detail more horrific, each time more people hurt, each way worse and worse and yet each conflict with its own specific history, many of them histories that we allowed to be formed while we enjoyed the touch of each others in the night.

But the more I look at the pattern of the clouds from our bed in the morning, the more it seems the world is spinning in some way that I can't understand.

Oh this endless twentieth century.

Oh endless.

Oh century.

Oh when will it end.

In recent days, I hear rumors that ships are being fueled and then are slipping out of port slowly at night.

I hear rumors from mothers in the street talking to other mothers.

I hear rumors from lovers in line at the grocery talking among themselves.

I hear rumors from friends at parties

I hear rumors of ships refueling and of ships slipping out of port while we sleep in our bed, even as I can't see them in the news.

In the news I learn that Iraq is ready for war but most people there are too busy to notice the refueling of ships here in my corner of the world and their beginning of that long journey to their corner of the world.

Even as I can't see the refueling of ships I see ten killed in the Bureij refugee camp by shells from Israeli tanks on Thursday and then one more killed in Gaza on Sunday and then five in east Nepal by a bomb that might have been set by Maoists and then one hundred and twenty in Monoko-Zohi by various means because of civil war.

Beloveds, how can we understand it at all?

Oh how can the patterns stop.

All I know is that I couldn't get out of bed anymore at all without yous in my life.

And I know that my ties with yous are not unique.

That each of those one hundred and thirty-six people dead by politics' human hands over the weekend had numerous people who felt the same way about them.

Chances are that each of those one hundred and thirty-six people dead by politics' human hands had lovers like I have yous who slipped yours hands between their thighs and who thought when their lovers did this that this is all that matters in the world yet still someone somewhere tells ships to refuel and then to slip out of port in the night.

Chances are that each of those one hundred and thirty-six people dead by politics' human hands had parents and children with ties so deep that those parents and children feel fractured now, one or two days later, immersed in a pain that has an analogy only to the intensity of pleasure.

Chances are that each of those one hundred and thirty-six people dead by politics' human hands had pets and plants that need watering. Had food to make and food to eat. Had things to read and notes to write. Had enough or had too little. Had beautiful parts and yet also had scars and rough patches of skin. Had desire and had impotence. Had meannesses, petty and otherwise. Had moments of kindness. Were nurtured for years by someone who was so devoted to them that they sacrificed huge parts of themselves to this nurturing and who today feel this loss of what they nurtured so intensely as to find their world completely meaningless today and will for some time after today.

And yet still someone somewhere tells ships to refuel and then to slip out of port in the night.

And it doesn't even end there.

The Greenland glaciers and Arctic Sea ice melt at unprecedented levels and still a ship fuels up and slips out of port.

Winona Ryder has thirty prescriptions for downers from twenty different doctors and still a ship fuels up and slips out of port.

Marc Anthony and Dayanara Torres renew their vows in Puerto Rico and still a ship fuels up and slips out of port.

Light and aromatherapy might help treat dementia, a patient sues a surgeon who left in the middle of surgery to pay his bills, cruise passengers continue to have diarrhea and nausea and yet continue to go on cruises, fires burn in Edinburgh, Hussein apologizes for invading Kuwait, United Airlines continues to lose eight million a day, Mars might have been a cold, dry planet when it was first formed, the Cheeky Girls knock Eminem off the charts, and still a ship fuels up and slips out of port.

January 13, 2003

Beloveds, I haven't been able to write for days.

I've just been watching.

Days ago North Korea unsealed its nuclear weapons reactors.

Days ago troops were moved into various positions. Gathered at various borders.

I traveled around the East Coast of the American continent hoping it would never begin but watching it begin at the same time.

We did not speak about it.

We talked on the phone from various locations and we used soft voices and spoke of loneliness and being apart and difficulties in sleeping and the coldness of our beds at night and then went on about our days and listed in great detail all its mundane troubles— missing staplers, cars driving too fast, endless snow, difficulties in getting fresh vegetables in the neighborhood—and we did not speak about it.

We did not speak about the December 24 deployment of twenty-five thousand soldiers, sailors, airmen, and marines to the Gulf Region.

We do not speak about the loading of M1 Abrams tanks, Apache helicopter gunships, and other equipment on two roll-on/roll-off ships, the *Mendonca* and the *Gilliland*, in Savannah, Georgia.

We do not speak about the *Seay* loaded with Patriot antimissile batteries and wheeled vehicles in Fort Bliss, Texas.

We do not speak about the *Constellation* in the Persian Gulf and the *Harry S. Truman* in the Mediterranean each with forty fighter jets on board, including F/A-18 Hornets and F-14 Tomcats, and about forty other aircraft.

We do not speak about the thousand-bed hospital ship *Comfort* that has left Baltimore for Diego Garcia and is waiting for orders.

And today, I am back with yous, beloveds, and still we do not speak about yesterday's deployment of sixty-two thousand soldiers, sailors, airmen, and marines to the Gulf Region that included seventeen thousand and five hundred marines and pilots, mechanics and additional warplanes, combat engineers, logistics support and loading crews.

What we heard as rumor a few weeks ago has become a listing in the daily news.

An endless refueling and slipping out of port in the night.

We do not speak of it and instead press up against one anothers reveling in the pleasure of being back together.

Some say thronging cavalry, some say foot soldiers, others call a
fleet.

Some say an army of cavalry, others of infantry, others of ships.

Some say horsemen or footmen or rowers.

Or a troop of horses, the serried ranks of marchers, a noble fleet,
some say.

Some say one hundred and twenty Challenger Two tanks, or
infantry, or a fleet of ships.

There are those who say a host of cavalry, M1A2 Abrams tanks,
and others Bradley fighting vehicles.

Some say others of infantry, and others of ships, and others of
155 mm Howitzers.

Some say thronging Warrior combat vehicles, some say foot soldiers,
others call a fleet the most beautiful of sights the dark earth offers.

Some say that the fairest thing upon the dark earth is a host of antiarmor AH-64 Apache attack helicopters, and others again a fleet of ships.

Some say that the most beautiful thing upon the black earth is an army of AS90 self-propelled guns, others infantry, still others ships.

On this dark earth, some say the thing most lovely is the thirty thousand assault troops from Britain today joining the sixty-two thousand from the US mobilized in the past ten days and a further sixty thousand from the US on their way.

On this black earth, over the coal-black earth, some say all of this and more.

But I say it's whatever you love best.

I say it is the persons you love.

I say it is those things, whatever they are, that one loves and desires.

I say it's what one loves.

It's what one loves, the most beautiful is whomever one loves.

I say it is whatsoever a person loves.

I say for me it is my beloveds.

For me naught else, it is my beloveds, it is the loveliest sight.

I say the sight of the ones you love.

I say it again, the sight of the ones you love, those you've met and those you haven't.

I say it again and again.

Again and again.

I try to keep saying it to keep making it happen.

I say it again, the sight of the ones you love, those you've met and those you haven't.

January 28, 2003

Yesterday the UN report on weapons inspections was released.

Today Israel votes and the death toll rises.

Four have died in clashes in the West Bank town of Jenin.

Yesterday, three died in an explosion at a Gaza City house.

Since last Monday US troops have surrounded eighty Afghans and killed eighteen.

Protests against the French continue in the Ivory Coast.

Nothing makes any sense today beloveds.

I wake up to a beautiful, clear day.

A slight breeze blows off the Pacific.

It is morning and it is amazing in its simple morningness.

I leave the house early so I miss the parrots but outside the door I stop to listen to the ugly song of the red-bottomed bulbuls.

It is so calm here and yet so momentous in the rest of the world.

Amid ignorant armies and darkling plains, the news has momentarily stopped trying to make sense and the stories appear with a doubleness.

Israel said the four killed today were armed men and were killed in a series of clashes.

Palestine claims they were shot in running battles.

Palestine claims the bomb explosion in Gaza was caused by a missile from an Israeli helicopter.

Israel claims it was a Palestinian bomb that exploded prematurely.

In the Ivory Coast some schoolboys sing, "France for the French, Ivory Coast for the Ivorians. Everyone go home. We are xenophobes and so what."

Others carry signs that say "Down with France, long live the US" and "No more French, from now on we speak English" and sing "USA, USA, USA" against the French.

Later today Bush will speak.

How can we be true to one another with histories of place so deep, so layered we can't begin to sort through it here in the middle of the Pacific with its own deep unsortable history?

I left our small apartment that is perched at the side of a dormant volcano that goes miles down to the ocean floor, perched on layer after layer of exploding history.

It wasn't just our history of place but the contradiction of the US taking unilateral military action to rid Iraq of its weapons of mass destruction that entered our two small rooms and we just wanted to leave and get on with the day's mundanenesses—email and photocopies and desk chairs and telephones.

While driving away from our small apartment, beloveds, I turned on the radio.

Today on the radio, Christie Brinkley exists and her worries about Billy Joel's driving abilities exist.

A lawsuit exists where Catherine Zeta Jones and Michael Douglas are suing *Hello!* magazine for publishing poor-quality wedding photos.

U2 spy planes exist flying over the Koreas.

Supermodel Gisele Bundchen's plan to eradicate hunger in Brazil exists.

Heart disease in women exists.

John Malvo's trial exists.

Aretha Franklin exists and a subpoena for her exists.

Hackers of the Recording Industry Association of America website exist.

Thalidomide exists.

Zoe Ball exists.

And Fatboy Slim exists but now without Zoe Ball.

Bronze Age highways in Iraq, Syria, and Turkey continue to exist.

Renée Zellweger and Richard Gere, lead actors in *Chicago*, exist.

Cell phones and tunnel vision exist.

Cable problems exist in a crash in Charlotte.

A dismembered mother, the shoe bomber's letters, Scott Peterson's wife and girlfriend, Brian Patrick Regan's letters to Hussein and Gadhafi, nineteen thousand gallons of crude oil in the frozen Nemadji River, all of this exists.

The world goes on and on, spins tighter and then looser on a wobbling axis, and it has a list of adjectives to describe it, such as various and beautiful and new, but neither light, nor certitude, nor peace exist.

February 15, 2003

Here is today.

Over eight million people marched on five continents against
the mobilization.

Here is today.

Three million in Rome.

Two million in Spain.

One and a half million in London.

Half a million in Berlin.

The list goes on.

Millions.

And if not millions then hundreds of thousands.

People in London, Dublin, Edinburgh, Reykjavik, Paris, Berlin, Leipzig, Stuttgart, Amsterdam, Brussels, Madrid, Seville, Andalusia, Barcelona, Girona, Granada, Rome, Bern, Stockholm, Gothenburg, Warsaw, Lisbon, Porto Codex, Bucharest, Moscow, Athens, Thessaloniki, Budapest, Helsinki, Ankara, Kiev, Belgrade, Sarajevo, Istanbul, Cape Town, Johannesburg, Jerusalem, Tel Aviv, Amman, Beirut, Rafah, Ramallah, Karachi, Lahore, Rawalpindi, Babylon, Baghdad, Bombay, Calcutta, Delhi, Srinagar, Hong Kong, Dili, Kuala Lumpur, Manila, Jakarta, Seoul, Bangkok, Damascus, Canberra, Newcastle, Melbourne, Sydney, Auckland, Christchurch, Wellington, Calgary, Buenos Aires, Rosario, Bogotá, Mexico City, Guadalajara, Santo Domingo, Guatemala City, Tegucigalpa, Anchorage, Arcata, Fresno, Los Angeles, Sacramento, San Francisco, San Jose, Santa Monica, Vallejo, Portland, Santiago, Lima, Caracas, Chicago, Normal, Detroit, Lansing, Minneapolis, Las Vegas, Santa Fe, Austin, Salt Lake City, Bellingham, Seattle, Tacoma, Toronto, Raleigh, Philadelphia, Ottawa, Quebec, Brasilia, Rio de Janeiro, São Paulo, Quito, Montevideo, San Jose, San Juan, Havana, gathered.

Even those on Antarctica gathered together.

Even we on this small island gathered.

Of course other things happened.

Dolly the cloned sheep was killed yesterday owing to premature aging.

A bomb exploded an Israeli tank and four were killed.

Cardinal Etchegaray visited Saddam Hussein but neither would say what they discussed.

Child protection campaigners called for the removal of Polanski's *The Pianist* from the Oscars because of the fugitive director's child sex conviction.

But mainly people gathered.

When I wake up this morning the world is a series of isolated,
burning fires as it is every morning.

It burns in Israel where ten died from a bomb on a bus.

Yesterday it also burned in the Philippines where twenty-one died
from a bomb at an airport. And then it burned some more a few
hours later outside a health clinic in a nearby city, killing one.

It burns and the pope urges everyone to fast and pray for peace
because it is Ash Wednesday.

It burns in Cambodia, which has closed its border with Thailand.

It burns in a fistfight between delegates at the Islamic emergency
summit.

It burns in the West Bank and the Gaza Strip.

It burns in the form of Israeli-imposed closures that cause severe
economic problems for Palestinians.

It burns in North Korea.

This is the stuff of the everyday in this world.

In this never-ending twentieth-century world.

This burning, this dirty air we breathe together, our dependence on this air, our inability to stop breathing, our desire to just get out of this world and yet there we are taking the burning of the world into our lungs every day where it rests inside us, haunting us, making us twitch and turn in our bed at night despite the comfort we take from each other's bodies.

Beloveds, weeks ago the doubleness of the news broke me down and I stopped writing and stopped loving all humans, mainly myself.

Heriberto wrote in his blog that US citizens should leave like German citizens should have left Nazi Germany.

I spent days thinking on this one.

Whether we could do anything here with others.

Or whether it was better for all of us to leave the nation to whatever strange fever has overtaken it.

The unanswerable questions of political responsibility.

The call to act despite the lack of answers.

As I thought about this, life went on.

As I thought, the shuttle crashed on its return home, North Korea restarted its plutonium reactors, two close friends broke up, another tried to kill himself, another checked himself out of rehab for the third time in order to return to his ice habit, and water continued to be wantonly used despite warnings that a lack of water will probably lead to severe crop shortages across the globe in the near future.

Beloveds, before all my hope is burnt up, I should also remember that eleven million people across the globe took to the streets one recent weekend to protest the war and this gave us all a glimmer.

We talked on the phone about this glimmer.

We read each other's reports.

We said optimistic things.

Those who broke up suddenly discovered new lovers and their new sensualities in this glimmer despite all the burning.

Friends got arrested for posting signs and they were suddenly heroes.

After the protests, I flip through as many images from as many different cities as I can find on the Internet.

Picture after picture, crowd after crowd.

The images differ only in the surroundings.

City streets or town squares; bright light of heat or the clear light of snow; naked or clothed protestors; mittens or halters.

Those on the space shuttle sent back images of the calm quietness of the planet before they crashed.

Those images give the comfort of distance, a lack of detail.

These images of the protests are busy, detailed with all the glimmers of individuals.

There are crowds covering blocks of city streets and squares, taken from above.

I imagine the bodies of friends in the crowds of various cities, feel moments of connection with the mass as I imagine it down to individuals.

March 11, 2003

Beloveds, the UN resolutions and counter-resolutions have
become so endless that I can't make sense of them anymore.

One day Turkey will not open its doors to US troops, the next day
there is an election and negotiations start all over again.

Our hopes that the inevitable will not come true are endlessly
dashed.

Bush keeps saying he will go it alone if he has to.

Huge protests continue, protests without alone and against alone.

It is the word alone, beloveds, the word alone.

When I speak of alone I speak of how there is no alone as Pakistan
claims it is moving in on bin Laden, as Iran's nuclear plant is
nearing completion, as Oscar organizers announce that the show
will go on in the event of war.

I speak of how there is no alone even with fuel cells and the deloder worm and the car lover's brain.

I speak of David Letterman's shingles, which he got from someone else.

Even the Broadway musicians are on strike together.

There is no alone as the Sri Lankan Navy sinks a Tamil Tiger ship and eleven are killed.

There is no alone in the food shortage in North Korea and Bush apologizing to Karzai.

It is an uneventful day overall as we sit here waiting for the news.

The television promises updates on the situation with Iraq on the half hour.

Our apartment is small and is buried between two other apartments, one above and one below.

Beloveds, my desire is to hunker down and lie low, lie with yous in beds and bowers, lie with yous in resistance to the alone, lie with yous night after night.

But the military-industrial complex enters our bed at night.

We sleep with levels of complicity so intense and various that our dreams are of smothering and drowning and of the military outside our door and we find it hard to get up in the morning.

I try to comfort myself with images of exile on this small piece of land in the middle of the large Pacific.

That view from space, this view now that seems so without promise, so empty of hope.

But I know there is no alone anymore here in the middle of the Pacific.

There is no uninhabited tropical island anywhere.

We live, after all, on the gathering isle.

Oh this disrupted center with all its occupied forces.

Oh the thirty Navy and Coast Guard warships docked on the shore of this island.

Oh the eighteen nuclear submarines docked on the shore of this island.

Oh the five destroyers docked on the shore of this island.

Oh the two frigates docked on the shore of this island.

Oh this on the map, off the map feeling.

March 16, 2003

In the last few days I have watched mynas gathering materials for their nests.

Yesterday I saw one pick up and carry off a big clump of dried grass.

And then I saw another struggling with a big piece of napkin at the side of the road.

Such optimism, beloveds, such optimism.

We went to the beach yesterday not in optimism but in avoidance and spoke about the birds around us and their constant singing of small songs, some of them ugly to us and some of them beautiful.

We were just talking because we could.

Because we could spend this time together in the sun and we knew that was something that mattered but as we spoke of birdsong we also spoke of Bush's summit Sunday with the leaders of Britain,

Spain, and Portugal in the Azores, and the prediction that there was a less than 1 percent chance of avoiding war.

When we spoke of birds and their bowers and their habits of nest we also spoke of the Israeli military bulldozer that ran over Rachel Corrie, the mysterious flu that appeared in Hong Kong and had spread by morning to other parts of Asia, Elizabeth Smart's return, and Zoran Djindjic's death.

We reclined as we spoke, we reclined and the sand that coated our arms and legs is known for a softness that is distinctive in the islands and the waves were a gentle one to three feet and a soft breeze blew through the ironwoods and we were surrounded by ditches, streams, and wetland areas, which serve as a habitat for endangered waterbird species.

There are other sorts of beauty on this globe, but this sort of beauty is fully realized here.

This sort of beauty cannot get any more beautiful, any more detailed, any more rich or perfect.

But the beach on which we reclined is occupied by the US military so every word we said was shaped by other words, every moment of beauty occupied.

We watched the planes fly overhead from the nearby airbase as we spoke of birds and their bowers and their habits of nest and we were also speaking of rolling start and shock and awe and two hundred and twenty-five thousand American forces and another ninety thousand on the way and twenty-five thousand British forces and one thousand Air Force, Navy, and Marine Corps combat and support aircraft in the area.

And because the planes flew overhead when we spoke of the cries of birds our every word was an awkward squawk that meant also AH-64 Apache attack helicopter, UH-60 Black Hawk troop helicopter, M2A3 Bradley fighting vehicle, M1A1 Abrams main battle tank, F/A-16 Hornet fighter/bomber, AV-8B Harrier fighter jet, AH-1W Super Cobra attack helicopter and that soon would mean other things also, the names of things still arriving, the B-2 stealth bombers from Whiteman Air Force Base, the B-52 bombers that are now in Britain.

March 17, 2003

We slept soundly during the night, beloveds, and when I woke yous were wrapped around me and I thought it was this that had let me dream of windows and doors opening and light entering, a relief from my recent dreams that have been so full of occupations.

But we wake up and all we hear in the birds' songs is war.

When the birds sing outside our window they sing of the end of negotiations with the UN, of the Dow soaring on confidence of a short war, of how rebel forces in the Central African Republic have dissolved parliament and suspended the constitution, of the resumption of the trading in oil futures in London after protestors broke into the building and fights broke out on the trading pit.

They sing of how someone makes Natalie Maines apologize for her shame that the president of the United States is from Texas, of seven people, killed in Palestine, of drug-resistant pneumonia that continues to spread, and of the worldwide mourning for Rachel Corrie.

The birds also sing of how celebrities in Los Angeles are getting their manicures and their hair done as they always do.

March 27 and 30, 2003

During the bombing, beloveds, our life goes on as usual.

Oh the gentle pressing of our bodies together upon waking.

Oh the parrots and their squawking.

Oh the soft breeze at five to ten miles per hour.

Oh the harsh sun and the cool shade.

Oh the papaya and yogurt with just a little salt for breakfast.

Oh the cool shower that we take together.

This makes us feel guiltier and more unsure of what to do than
ever.

We watch it all happen on television.

We go to protests as they happen.

We write up reports of our protests and send them out to friends who then send them on to friends and we read the reports of others with pleasure and hope.

We count numbers attending and numbers arrested.

This weekend . . .

one hundred in Sanaa

five hundred in New Delhi

fifty thousand in Athens

ten thousand in Cape Town

twenty-five thousand in Boston

one thousand and five hundred in Chicopee

three thousand in Los Angeles

three thousand in Santiago

one hundred and twenty thousand across Australia

one hundred in Beijing

ten thousand in Edinburgh

ten thousand in Paris

fifty thousand in Berlin

thirty thousand between the cities of Osnabrück and Münster

and then others in Cairo, Amman, Jakarta

in Brussels, in Athens

in San Francisco, New York, and Chicago.

Still a huge sadness overtakes us daily because of our inability to
control what goes on in the world in our name.

And we comment on the pleasures of our own lives sardonically to try to take back this sadness, these nightmares that happen in the world while we are sleeping and show up in our dreams, pinning us down to the bed, on our backs squawking.

We say ironic things to each other.

Oh go get your war on we say when one is being too boastful.

Oh sure, we say, oh yeah, we say over and over while watching some general talk about something, as if mocking inarticulate expressions of dissatisfaction from our childhood will save us.

Today, as this war begins, every word we say is caught—every word, whether it is ironic or not, whether it is articulate or not—and we feel it all in the room all day long.

When we speak of Lisa Marie Presley having sex with Michael Jackson we speak of JDAM and JSOW air-to-surface precision bombs.

We speak of the stinger antiaircraft missiles and the massive ordnance air-blast bombs when we speak of SAP AG and the Microsoft RPC hole and the Denial of Service attacks.

When we mumble about whether the mystery disease is a statutory communicable disease or not we can't keep the words M1A1 Abrams battle tanks, M2A3 Bradley fighting vehicles, M6 Bradley linebackers, and Humvees from stumbling out of our mouths.

When we speak of Robert Blake back in court we speak of GBU laser-guided bombs, of GBU-28 bunker buster bombs.

We speak of Daisy Cutter fifteen-thousand-pound bombs as we speak of both the MK82 five-hundred- and two-thousand-pound bombs and we also speak of thermobaric weapons, Tomahawk/AGM-86 cruise missiles, and Have Nap missiles when we speak of Snoop Dogg's decision to include in his latest song a message left on his answering machine by Big Jim Bob that taunts Suge Knight.

When we talk about how the Florida nurse died of the smallpox vaccination and how sperm may sniff their way to eggs we talk also of M109A6 Paladin Howitzers and the M270 multiple-launch rocket system.

We get up in the morning and the words "Patriot missile systems," "the Avengers," and "the US infantry weapons" tumble out of our mouths before breakfast.

When we marvel at the new one-hundred-billion-dollar theater for Celine's new show at Caesar's Palace we marvel also at the maverick air-to-surface missiles, the HARM antiradar missiles, the AIM-120 air-to-air missiles, and the Hellfire air-to-surface missiles.

And it goes on and on all day long and then we go to bed.

In bed, when I stroke the down on yours cheeks, I stroke also the carrier battle group ships, the guided missile cruisers, and the guided missile destroyers.

When I reach for yours waists, I reach for bombers, cargo, helicopters, and special operations.

When I wrap around yours bodies, I wrap around the *USS Abraham Lincoln*, unmanned aerial vehicles, and surveillance.

When I rest my head upon yours breasts, I rest upon the *USS Kitty Hawk* and the *USS Harry S. Truman* and the *USS Theodore Roosevelt*.

Guided missile frigates, attack submarines, oilers, and amphibious transport/dock ships follow us into bed.

Fast combat support ships, landing crafts, air cushioned, all of us with all of that.

DESIGNER: SANDY DROOKER
TEXT: ADOBE GARAMOND
DISPLAY: AKZIDENZ GROTESK
PRINTER AND BINDER: FRIESENS CORPORATION